COMMONS

NEW CALIFORNIA POETRY

EDITED BY	Robert Hass
	Calvin Bedient
	Brenda Hillman

COMMONS

Myung Mi Kim

University of California Press

Berkeley   Los Angeles   London

University of California Press
Berkeley and Los Angeles, California

University of California Press, Ltd.
London, England

© 2002 by The Regents of the University of California

Library of Congress Cataloging-in-Publication Data

Kim, Myung Mi, 1957–
Commons / Myung Mi Kim.
    p.   cm. — (New California Poetry ; 5)
ISBN 978-0-520-23144-3 (pbk. : alk. paper)
1. Korean Americans — Poetry.   2. Immigrants —
Poetry.   3. Korea — Poetry.   I. Title.   II. Series.

PS3561.I414 C66 2002
811'.54 — dc21   2001048053
                                            CIP

Manufactured in the United States of America

14   13   12   11   10   09   08   07
11   10   9   8   7   6   5   4   3

CONTENTS

ACKNOWLEDGMENTS

Some of these poems first appeared in *Chain, Conjunctions, Five Fingers Review, non, positions: east asia cultures critique,* and *Proliferations.*

EXORDIUM

In what way names were applied to things. Filtration. Not every word that has been applied, still exists. Through proliferation and differentiation. Airborn. Here, this speck and this speck you missed.

Numbers in cell division. Spheres of debt. The paradigm's stitchery of unrelated points. What escapes like so much cotton batting. The building, rather, in flames. Does flight happen in an order.

Dates to impugn and divulge. The laws were written on twelve tablets of bronze which were fastened to the rostra. Trembling hold. Manner of variation and shift. Vacillation hung by tactile and auditory cues.

Those which are of foreign origin. Those which are of forgotten sources. Place and body. Time and action. The snow falls. A falling snow. A fallen snow. A red balloon and a blackwinged bird at semblance of crossing in a pittance of sky.

Chroniclers enter texts and trade. Was to children dying before their mothers. Accounts and recounting. A nation's defense. Names of things made by human hands. Making famine where abundance lies.

Mapping needles. Minerals and gems. Furs and lumber. Alterations through the loss or transposition of even a single syllable. The next day is astronomical distance and a gnarled hand pulling up wild onion.

Placed on a large flat rock and covered by a series of smaller stones. Edicts of building for private persons. Remaining principalities long ago divided off. Under that place which is called the earth wall. Around which extends a savage, trackless waste, infested with wild beasts.

Near city walls. Shapes of battle helmets. Instruments for giving precision to ideas of size, distance, direction, and location. A projection of the possible state. Lay bare and make appear. The gates are wicked — fresh.

With shields. For war and fields. This hill was previously called — it is recorded that on this hill — When the rickshaw stopped, it was three o'clock. The heavy chains were taken off and they walked to the place of execution. One boy's shoe fell off, and he reached down to put it back on, taking a long time to do it. Fierce dogs have come over the sea.

Cutworms in tomato beds. Roots of a tree close to the property line have gone out under the neighbor's cornfield. Wherever kin of word is. Partnership of words is one of many members.

Glyphs to alphabets. In which words have indications of time. They had to eat as much as they could in a hurry. Baskets woven by bloodlet fingers.

Venom verifies. Minuscule pebbles embedded in domestic crops. With the soot covered rice pot — stood and sat, stood and sat, several times. Meals offered up from yet more pinecones burning.

A second class of words in which comparisons are made. The pond after rain, a lily. Watershed and water level. Coinciding glint of scales and scrapers. Conjectural poles.

Speaking and placing the speaking. To speak from the place of the word is to speak forth. Such noise in the ditches — the mills and farms.

Standing in proximity — *think* and *love*. See, meet, face. Incidence of generation. Walls of wattles, straw, and mud. A laundering stone and stones for the floor. Gently, gently level the ground. This is the leveling of the ground.

LAMENTA

229

318

The transition from the stability and absoluteness of the world's contents
to their dissolution into motions and relations.

P: Of what use are the senses to us — tell me that

E: To indicate, to make known, to testify in part

Burning eye seen

Of that

One eye seen

bo-bo-bo   *k-k-k*

Jack-in-the-pulpit   petaling

To a body of infinite size there can be ascribed neither center nor boundary

say   .   siphon

Sign scarcity, the greeting — *have you eaten today?*

Signal of peonies   singing given to bullfrogs

Give ear to the quarrels of the marketplace

When the wheel (A) was turned, the gate (B) was raised, thus allowing water to flow from (C) to (D), giving clearance for the ship to pass beneath

lever   .   girt

Host and parasite

Implicated armed band

Where would one live

A custom of wrapping the head in willow branches

311

Hours whose length varied with seasons

Hours held by mechanical clock

An abstract metric to gauge daily time

Compendium to dispersals of currency

Farm and factory, bank and municipality

travel   .   athwart

What would identify the speakers of the idiom

312

Woodness and continual waking

Raging stretching and casting

Now chanting now weeping

The medicine is that the head be shaved, washed in lukewarm vinegar

The forehead anointed with the juice of lettuce or of poppy

If the woodness lasts three days without sleep, there is no hope of recovery

"war-torn"

"turbulent homeland"

All that we see could also be otherwise

All that we can describe could also be otherwise

The thing seen is the thing seen together with the whole space

314

Wakeful works under weeds (wed)

Tell a poor play

Money and mourning met

Sun and sorrow am sent

For fade and flame

Between March and April when spray begin to spring

As apples two of dread

Ourselves mowen so

Wild drakes make whom them bind

False nerve on hours red

Reeds which lie in fold

So harms hinges bore

To be at this thinking trod

Pray of love, one full keen

Why are many buildings necessary with so small a farm area?

The heat of the midday sun is obvious, but the pressure of populations on the inadequate areas of flat land has to be inferred.

For the flock, a brief flash announces possible food

mite   a copper coin of very small value
            a small weight
            a minute particle or portion

detent   stop or catch in a machine which prevents motion and the removal of which
            brings some motor into immediate action (as in guns, clocks, watches)

deterge   to wash off or out, to clear away foul or offensive matter from the body

s-s-s

how to false bottom log
whom I saw beautiful as a boy

nuph-juk-pahn
nubh-jjuk-paan

shun   .   nestle

ravenous   .   seal

ash   .   gust

317

— to settle refugees — to remove land mines
And their task leaked

cho-gah-jiib : a color — straw and wintered grass

The question is labor
Skin loosening from bone is age

Ages longer than drought or rain

Grafted

ee . 으
ㄴ

318

Their [brilliance and their dependence]

Flowers [gladiolas, zinnia, delphinium]

Offset the houses

What the bluejay exacts [upside down]
[inside] the half-broken sunflower, pecking

Scrip — a small purse carried by a pilgrim, shepherd, or beggar

One among fled many
                felt

Any different tissue constitutes a heterology

White light after breath (circling the mouth)//

The baby asleep in the house
And two figures down by the barn

It burns. Membrane.

Further carbonization of matter

bellrag   ス
bellslip   jw

319

405

322

Terms stringent for lack of food

Root insect berry pass a mud inscription

Place where

Weeks of slaughter and remonstrance

Fed the children and animals first

Without interruption the entry log of days

Snow may be falling

VOCALISE

"the woman I had anatomized in the past year, or A.D. 1315, in the month of March had a uterus

"twice as large as one whom I anatomized in the month of January in the same year . . . And because

"the uterus of a pig which I anatomized in A.D. 1306 was a hundred times larger than it can ever

"be seen in a human being, there may be another cause, i.e., because it was pregnant and had

"in the uterus 13 little pigs. In this I showed the anatomy of the fetus or of pregnancy

324

is that green the willow grove

flowers color river hamlets

call of (the) cuckoo

through brushwood gate

tree-root mushrooms

almost (forget) forgotten fish

narrowness (width) of the angler's boat

the span of the world (earth)

painted screen of mossy rocks

how many crows have just flown over(head)

beat time on the sailmast

what is to be thought of long years spent fishing

stocky purplish stalks, the white flowers they put (out)

MASK PLAY

Father Mask

Mother Mask

Sister Mask

Marriage is Arranged Mask

Funeral Mask

Wedding Mask

Man Mask

Vagina Mask

Hemorrhage Mask

328

I stayed alive and listened

Orifices mercury and sulfur

So close ill

sever . thrift

Translucence of cut pears on glass plates

The robin's breast remained inert. Its eyes shone for four hours, but near three o'clock, a fly could be seen rubbing its legs over the now weeping eye.

401

Alteration in condition or fortune

The armory is approachable from the relative east and southeast

A directory of waste

From the practice of accommodating

Thus rang to the washstand, the birthing chair, and the crematory

To be added to the store of the human

Motion: that which refuses to be annihilated

402

Lifts up his burning

A stranger now   a stranger in my clean head

Strokes of green and purple is crocus

Sepal : gape

404

Her name and her mother's name
Her name and her sister's name

Carcass of coyote and deer separated by a stream linked by bones

sk - sk

Meaning the spectator part of the theatre but also, stall, birdcage, beehive

sahl-rlim-sah-ri   house
                         chores

VOCALISE

"On the 23rd of July of that year, I had taken a dog in good condition and well fed,

"for a vivisection at the request of some of my friends, who very much wanted to see

"the recurrent nerves. When I finished this demonstration of the nerves, it seemed

"good to watch the movements of the diaphragm in the same dog, at the same operation.

"While I was attempting this, and for that purpose had opened the abdomen and was

"pulling down with my hand the intestines and stomach gathered together into a mass,

"I suddenly beheld a great number of cords as it were, exceedingly thin and beautifully

"white, scattered over the whole of the mesentery and the intestine, and starting from

"almost innumerable beginnings. But presently, I saw that I was mistaken in this since

"I noticed that the nerves belonging to the intestine were distinct from these cords,

"and wholly unlike them, and besides, were distributed quite separately from them.

"Wherefore, struck by the novelty of the thing

De Fabrica Humani Corporis, Vesalius, 1543

405

periplus   voyage around a coastline or the narrative of such a voyage

muo   the fifty-fifth term in the cycle of sixty used to count years, months, days, and hours

The fundamental tenet of all military geography is that every feature of the visible world possesses actual or potential military significance

Little flower,

What day is it

The light stops at glum

O'clock and f

A rain saturated tree trunk becomes a feeling

The city of one's birth and the people inside it

406

424

406

pr

perdu   lying hidden, disguised. one who acts as a watcher or scout

perdure   to continue, endure, last on

The two are begun

They are shaving ends of sticks

The two are discussing seeds

They are specimens

Glass does not burn but the hillside does

The two are a vine's exhalation

409

Then follow wood then water, then stones and metals, slow to heat

bbi-du-πhuh-jut-dah   askew leaning twisted

In the bowels and studies of inferiors

Seaweed stench

410

[when my father died and left me nothing]

[this is how I speak]

412

"helicopters hover"
"embassy compound"

Relative fence, cling fence
Someone is hiding an infant

Fish with two tails
Fish with two heads

Indigestible over days and days

415

War is there and travel

The same is my sister, brothers, and mother

The father is thrush, white at birth and at dusk

Father is burying ground cool to the touch

This is some color but what color is it

"left their homes after two solid days of attacks"

"they had stayed to take care of their cow"

"the extreme cold froze medicine"

"religion and capitalism intersect in the muddy village twenty miles north of"

418

What started then and ate through most of a decade

The affliction is very near — and there is no one to help

The dead dog placed around my shoulders — weeds higher than my head

Standing as standing might

VOCALISE

"I have dissected more than ten human bodies, destroying all the various members

"and removing the minutest particles of flesh which surrounded these veins, without causing

"any effusion of blood . . . and as one single body did not suffice for so long a time,

"it was necessary to proceed by stages with so many bodies as would render my

"knowledge complete

The Notebooks, da Vinci

At least 250,000 acres of cotton and fruit crops are under immediate threat from the huge swarm of locusts which have invaded the southern plain from the Pamir Mountains

Roving simians have ripped the curtains off polling booths and pushed some officials preparing for parliamentary elections

In southwest and south-central Kansas the worst condition is plants stunted or killed off by extremely dry soil. Adding to farmers' woes are infestations of green bugs and brown wheat mites

Three villages were overrun by thousands of toads, and farmers in the area reportedly feel that the onslaught is a sign of impending tragedy. Children are said to be terrified by the toads and unable to sleep. The main road connecting the region with La Paz is coated with a thick layer of dead toads and the stench is said to be unbearable.

423

"peacekeeping troops"
"tanks beneath the windows"

The inside of someone else's dwelling visible — a table and some chairs.

You start to count one, two, three, four . . . until the explosion is near your neighborhood. You can guess the position of mortar by this counting and try to find a safe place.

If the windows are gone, weak plastic is taped up but the strong wind comes and we stay awake.

In this South Cholla Province where all vehicles had been confiscated, we resorted to walking, the method of travel of the Yi Dynasty. We reverted back 300 years.

Kwangju, 1980

It's the same to be in the house, at the shelter or anywhere. There is no safe place. When we have no electricity, we are sitting in the dark and we know what life looked like before Christ.

Sarajevo, 1992

424

The central organizing myth of comprehensive knowledge

Bent as light might bend

The openings in the human body

The age that one is

I will be my mother's age also

Color of robin's egg against spring grass

425

515

425

Any killing

Future passive

Campaign

Compound of, here

Take away

Think proper

After siege, used to dwell

Account of hard

Work, house with child, fear

Of marketplace, struck

Being made

Is

426

jiph-jiph-jiph

Swallow Swallow Bird

This is the gullet

Helmets make cooking pots

Tin cans make roofs

[sparrow, crow]

Not much left
Not much left

502

To bring to a close

What is to do
What is to happen

VOCALISE

"We found one girl about 12 or 13 years old standing in front of the hospital. Without

"any burns or apparent injury, she only complained of being thirsty. We didn't have any

"drinking water, so I gave her some gargle. The next day, I found her dead in the same

"spot. I didn't understand why she died. I can only surmise that her insides had imploded.

"Acute internal injuries and not one mark on her body. No one ever knew who she was

August 6, 1945

503

Salt rot

Bramble flesh

Litter husk

Blink ditch

Hunt stick

Hunger welt

Trow Song

$$\frac{ap}{ac}$$

Pock

ji-wuat-dah erased

jil-eu-dah shouted

Regarded among penury

Numb pie mum pie

jip-sae-gi *ji-pah-raeng-e* : show here

Look at that noise!

Numb pie mum pie

Abnormalities included growth retardation, fasciation, malformation, and variegation, with the latter being most prominent. As to variegation of leaves, the white portion took a linear, spotty, and cloudy form and turned completely white in extreme cases. The shade of white varied.

Unendurable, said one

cha-goph-dah, said one

flail   :   sounding

New buds did not sprout from the damaged side of trees within 700 meters of the hypocenter. Among the herbs that regenerated rapidly, there were sweet potato, taro, dwarf lily turf and big blue lily turf.

Sitting on haunches to perform everyday tasks on the order of trimming greens or rinsing clothes.

511

staunch . severance

s   *h*

How (would) the hills figure in

Acacia

As to water

512

Emperor:

Sacrificer:

Fish:

Old woman:

Swine:

Daughter:

Hand, thigh:

Strength, particle:

Strife and violence are harmful to a city. Each
is responsible for deaths. The old men said
the women must obey the laws, while the old
women said that the men had proven
responsible for evils to the city. Birds born
tail first. Weak cattle. In accordance with
misfortune. River full of sweet water. Fouled.
Our life is. Half died. Meteorite is a pebble
wedged in a dog's paw.

703

722

703

Pitches to mire

Growing objects on a hillside
Stems and rough outer barks

Bile   sediment

Obtuse   limited vocabulary while lying down

Grove bird   shellfish powder

Flowers and timberline proceed in relation

Spittle, bittle

Lup/ /lapiary

Peregrine's (*f l*)

      sumac

Muri   *dori*

As a head fit without torso

Throat in hand

A farmhouse and outbuildings
An open screen door

So we speak of marauding, flooding

706

for contralto

Enemies surround us

But even our own people

Have turned into leopards, lions, and wolves

Snatching anything that moves

Boils eat us up

712

Work the fields

March to war

Kill enough animals, find enough fruit, keep the family fed

Motion of the greater congregation

716

Grief would have so a mark

Wilt and mold

Diminishing possibility of cucumber and pole bean vine

Human face worn by animals

Avowal worried by use

Breakfall of nations

The gnawed pleasure boats

717

Stun . sun shaped

Rot and water molecule
Beach and infection

Mother: there are 150 stars as configuration in the apple. In the apparent core, fixities come off.

Father: the medicine was not in the bag. I did not understand why I was looking at the photo or rather, what it had to do with the rest of the wall.

It was made then . face an appear

What fattens the earth fattens eyes and eyelids

722

Each burgeoning . Violet . Gentian . Bluff attenuating light . Days as

marches . After, the sound was ratchety . Cherry hung branches . Hereditary marks .

Milk spout and tongue seal . Of living in the same dwelling . Was it a long time then —

Market value of melon . Harbinger would . Skin peeled back and thorax open .

Speculative germ . Apparition grass .

WORKS

Aggregate

Placed onto the actual
As in tool, scraper, shaper

Operative   *f* *fl*

A bereft

aba . *apa*

A small number multiplied many times by itself

A roof rises and absorbs
Detritus of moving waters

hand   .   motion

A chime has been hung

        (implied action
        (attenuated to broken action

Bloom   already in mark

So that it were a bloom

Steeped in increments

Marks   as were scars

[Longing Atlas]

Six grasses: rice wheat corn barley oats sorghum

Four legumes: soybeans peas beans peanuts

Five fruits: tomato grape apple orange mango

Abominations : (at) rest play sick

swarm . peck

In a dress and in a field

May . appeared . so does nesting

Spoke to us . spake

In a time of bee, honey, lavender

Woods were scrub and sapling

Weak arm of the flowering crabapple

Grown as a funnel

Speared

Test a direct experience of temperature

How harsh was that rest

Bottom feeders in habitual circle

m   fs

Broad Spectrum (intensive gathering)

Neolithic (farming)

Urban Revolution (rise of world economy)

That which is healthy and then again ill

sayings   .   rift

s   m

Of [names] of [things]   nose pike
                            single pike
                            bellow fin

Name of the [mother]   minutiae

How long have those swings been there

Siege Document

sesang sarămdŭr-a

세상 사람 들아

sae sahng sah rham deul ah

i nae mal tŭrŏ poso

이 네말 들어 보소

e nae mahl deul uh boh soh

naj-i myŏn-ŭn mur-i malkko

낯이 면은 물이 맑오

naht e myun eun nul e mahl ggo

pam-i myŏn-ŭn pur-i palga

밤이 면은 불이 발가

bahm e myun eun bul e bahl gah

ttae-nŭn mach'um onŭ ttae-nya?

때는 맡침 어느 때 냐?

ddae neun maht chim uh neu ddae nyah?

This time what time does it happen to be?

r   s

bandage pulled back is blood gone mud

þ   eu   hand hewn

freedom from commerce was a cry

filterdoubt   locution   .   string and pelter   .

apt screen   .   sake   .   contamination rat   .

attached to pillars and saltbeds

wracked as imperfect lot

Sleep took the eye muscle and severed it

In the vernacular   ate   stirred   swept

At the periphery   garbage pigs

: sandscroll :

After a long last

I learn my story

My mother had restaurant

She made noodle soup

It was famous soup

She suffer so much

For so much her life

It burn skin to bone

Scar tissue on top of nerve ending

Ugly power of military

I scream too hot too hot

Naked where clothes were a second before

signs and symptoms

crossing veins of lettuce and a miner's light

whose bones therefore appear short or thin relative to dental age

anemia recorded as porosity of the eye orbits

some by excess, some by defect

others by affliction

others by time for animals to be gathered together, time when water is drawn

(to) provide for days when hunting is poor or many are sick

The rest buried him by striking him with fir trees

Having consumed the eight sparrows in the nest

The wounded were washed in hot waters

Now the twentieth year since she quitted her native land

Exposure and desertion

: Many of the residents who have died of heat exhaustion were elderly men and women
reluctant to use air conditioning because they worried about expensive utility bills

Houseless heads and unfed sides

For the most part there is the smell of dried meat

Detail of blood smears

All at once the maggots were arrived

Capital   .   wound fragrant

Here are specimens   grit in the folds of greens

Direct pillage

Equal dispensation of dirt in the doorway

Compelled for the rest of the year to feed on noxious shoots

Cultivation rights

——————————
————————————
——————————
too bad

The lower level of the social hierarchy ===== made up of ==== who tilled and
=======the food

======== being atomized============ occurs
=========================== price lists ===========================
=====================

.   .

As they enter, they cut down grains, tear down the inner and outer walls, and fill up the
ditches and ponds; they exterminate the aged and the weak

In the calendars available, shortages are documented as a result of human actions: civil
wars, piracy, failure to transport food where needed

Sometimes they dug holes and ordered us to get into them

If you don't work
You don't eat

내일 부터 일하지 말아라
그러 캐도 생각 했지요

희망이 없어요

목이 멜 정도로

그러키 때문에

죽이 전에 한번

잊이 못할 내 고향이

식구 없이

한 40년도 됫이요 ──

얼마나 오래 동안

김 올가 할머니

The Elder Olga Kim
Siberia, 1992

My strength

As they have hacked off

Generation which is

Are stunted

Or pack animals

: I have nothing to say   I have nothing left to say   Glorious name

: Levels of aggregation may be extended in principle and without limit,
  multiple nested units between household and world

Hand lettered signs
Strung on twenty below temperatures

Severed thumbs in the boning room
A baseball sized bandage, was it?

The thing brought into genuineness

: has also found safety in the U.S. He's apparently a valued employee at Our Way, a compressor plant

: The second and fourth movements will use no speech whatsoever

: Debt burden does kill

Paltry did it

Paltry said so

skilter head   .   lifts up and tells simple mother stories

everyday to spout

everyday to alight

everyday to bring one end to the other, close

a pick a pack a frightening fund

that.   wants a biscuit

: I am assured that the global buying frenzy
: I am assured that there is a global buying frenzy

drain in a prophylactic sense

in plain sight cusp of flesh and action

that said: the cost

that said: brittle off the bone and perjure

Constant Reverential Face

Please allow that

Place of feet and water

Please allow that

The oil and seeds

What is the call to call out

⌐laughter visited us early and left⌐

moving around a sequence of debts

there would be the occasion of reaching for a foreign object in the eye

Speaker: She got shot. She did. I saw her.

limbs of pines rope around the waist

neither slaves nor freemen, but who have become part of the soil upon which they work
like so many cows and the trees

the schools had been burned down
 the teachers had been starved to death
the road had fallen into decay
the bridges were gone

will be eaten
at a ration of quarters
will be eaten
at a ration of fifths

For "lack" is said in many ways

That the raccoon has determined a path into the chicken coop

Caught in that snare that is her mother's terror

Afraid of that snare that iteration of terror the terror is her mother

Hair left a molecule disturbed

The plane fell in a direct line above the depressed area

Instruction platform made by heaping up earth and stones

The windows are missing the floor is fall through the smell is steam and mice

Possesses the eyes of a hawk, possessed of senses

We are allowed to keep one bag of potatoes or carrots after working a ten-hour day
pulling these vegetables and loading them onto trucks

The child ate two or more servings
The child asked for a simple plastic comb

Tuber   expectancy   ammonia

The point at which something is a ruin

Perforating scrawl

55 floods, 25 windstorms, 57 droughts, 37 plagues of locusts

: The amounts they speak of are in reality quite small and because of the missing
one hundred dollars everything they have could be put up for farm auction

Rudimentary sinew connecting library, school, and public land

Nine magnets on a scale of difference and citizenship

Disinfectant seeping into the carton of milk

The books were in the cellar

The backs of gated projects   the facade of the opera house

A theatre of operations: walking speaking eating brushing cooking folding

Ate cake   lost shoes   built boat   hid ax

The simple sugar inside a wasp   the liquid in sand

Bitter, bitter roots

water supply silted

children sold for token payment, for the promise that they would be fed

seasonal hunger

human cash crop

if to bend back at stems

also called horsetail, scouring rush

to set forward   work of the house

chapters of lily

intended in the branching

throstle

The sky also warned

"this is where we come from"

Being dark it was square grey houses in a barren land

Task and fruition

Foods cast off from one culture become the fetish foods of another

l   b

Speaker: There will be misery in the years of greed. The world will become small and humiliated.

what is folded, are the persimmons

what is shelled, are the chestnuts

The heap by which we know burnt children

Illumination's wick — mercy, grief

And the houses, provisional houses sprung up together, around each other, haphazard,
in a formation — in a form seeking shield from the wind

Someone had sorted the femurs

Corpse confused with a bolt of cloth

Sawing Song

t'opchil norae

The story is about a girl who does not know her name or her age

Mother who had gone to stay under earth
Father who had gone to stay under heaven

One day she sets out to look for her parents and meets a boy and girl called "Always" and "Everyday"

There lived millions and millions of poor and tired human beings, toiling like ants who have built a nest underneath a heavy stone. They worked for the benefit of someone else. They shared their food with the animals of the fields. They died without hope.

Hold this up

Amid listening board and gourd

Were to pipe and fittings

Free from function

To change the position of enunciation and the relations within it

Peregrine and Earth

The day that makes one an orphan

A wheel

A place of assembly

A ring or circle of people

Belonging to or used in processions

A solemn procession to a temple with singing and music

sayings   .   disturbances

A nation to be humanized

Visited by a humble pounding

The meaning of becoming related

This is to be done

This is to be sung

shambling   .   shambles

That snapdragon's crimson
Understood as a potential sound

Came at us   leapt

[*fm*]

this is]   this *is* light

this is]   this held all around

POLLEN FOSSIL RECORD

Book of Famine, Book of Attempt, Book of Money
Book of Labor, Book of Scribes
Book of Utterance, Book of Hollow Organs,
Book of Tending, Book of Wars, Book of Household,
Book of Protection, Book of Grief, Book as Inquiry

Swerves, oddities, facts, miscues, remnants — threnody and meditation —
the perpetually incomplete task of tracking what enters into the field of perception
(the writing act) — its variegated and grating musics, cadences, and temporalities

Book as specimen
Book as instruction

The book emerges through cycles of erosion and accretion

COMMONS elides multiple sites: reading and text making, discourses and disciplines,
documents and documenting. Fluctuating. Proceeding by fragment, by increment.
Through proposition, parataxis, contingency — approximating nerve, line, song

Velocity, the exultant and transitory glimpse of encounter

The inchoate and the concrete coincide

Desire for the encyclopedic // Interrogation of archive

Released into our moment, shaped as it is by geographical and cultural displacements, an exponentially hybrid state of nations, cultures, and voicings

Even in the midst of (or perhaps especially in view of) a fully entrenched commodity society, how might it be possible to render the infinitesimally divisible moment

The meaning of becoming a historical subject.

"Aphorisms are 'broken knowledge' that create 'wonder'," Advancement, *Bacon*

Because isolations occur

Uncover the ear

To give form to what is remote, castigated

The necessity of carving out [intuiting/enacting] one's own treatment of a particular arena of language

Social and psychic identifications that disrupt and (re)envision, to throw into question conventions of codifying

Form as interplay of mobile elements, actuated by the ensemble of movements developed within it

The comportment is one of experiment

The poem infiltrates, filters, avulses :   nuance and gradation

"The fragment is that part of the totality of the work that opposes totality." *Aesthetic Theory*, Adorno

The contrapuntal, the interruptive, the speculative

What is the work of household — the moral and just education of a child

The interrelation between populations and their environments

There is the discussion about shortages

A collapse in food production, socioeconomic differentiation, and poverty were the results

Social rules for distribution
Cultural rules for consumption

Feminization of poverty // Feminization of the problem of lived time

_____, a word that cannot be translated: it suggests, "what belongs to the people"

Modes, registers of   [collectivity

Human voice   range
               (to) bursting
               prayer

Sound's physicality   [human longing

Of being in and affecting

Poets as "agents for the most arduous, most dangerous cause there is: to love the other, even before being loved." *Stigmata*, Cixous

To usher in   : time action matter

"dates to impugn and divulge"

The daily and the continuous.

"Lamenta" attempts to hold in relation these two indicatives, fixed time and cyclical time.

Chronicling lived time : registering the continuum of history.

Structurally, responding to the idea of the Metonic cycle, a cycle of nineteen years, transposed (mutated?) to the daily and the materiality of history.

Bound time (chronology) up against radicalized time (mutability of chronology).

To call into question, to disclose, to make common

The idea of romanization

The ideas of translation, translatability, transliteration, transcription:

Bit, part, scattered phoneme, suggestion of sounds, a glitch of ear and tongue occurring in unrecognizable patterns: for a long time I dismissed (or couldn't fold in or hold) these random, skittish stutterings. However, once perceived as (made audible and tactile as) potential sounds in Korean or, for that matter, any number of languages (Middle English, Latin, French) that constitute "English," these roaming fragments fall into the writing. Yet, how to render their presence fully? Sometimes, this necessitated conjoining the English and Korean alphabets (ㅈ /jw) or (ee/ㅇ]).

Rehearsals of conflating Korean and English texts, for example, in the body of a 14th century *sijo* or an alliterative English poem from about the same time. Set in concurrent motion, these texts were "translated" simultaneously. It is not the actual translation or even the state of translatability between the two texts that is intriguing but the possibilities for transcribing what occurs in the traversal between the two languages (and, by extension, between the two "nations," their mutually implicated histories of colonization, political conflicts, and so on). What is the recombinant energy created between languages (geopolitical economies, cultural representations, concepts of community)?

Rehearsals of listening: practicing sound and gesture between languages, between systems of writing. How physically (almost physiologically) impossible it is to pronounce or even imagine what Korean words are being depicted under the standard (standardized) romanization of Korean. The odd vowel blurs, the unclear consonant combinations. Poised between a spectral and real engagement with Korean. The practicing had to be one in which this specific formulation of ear, mouth, and tongue had to find a correspondence in "English" — oral, aural, and written. Practices in transliteration: comparing the standard romanization to what [I] might be said to be hearing: "sesang sarămdŭr-a" next to "sae sahng sah rham deul ah." Whose ears are at work? Where does the authority of romanizing reside? How might it be entered into otherwise?

A further rehearsal: being compelled to write down as exactly as possible the words of Olga Kim, speaking about her forty years of living in Siberia, and knowing fully that an atrophied, arrested, third grade Korean writing is what was available. What was missing? What was forgotten? What was never learned in the first place? What was and was not written "correctly"? Each of these instances is enunciative.

These rehearsals, not as description, but as activation — actively investigating how legibility is constructed and maintained, how "English" is made and disseminated.

What *is* English now, in the face of mass global migrations, ecological degradations, shifts and upheavals in identifications of gender and labor? How can the diction(s), register(s), inflection(s) as well as varying affective stances that have and will continue to filter into "English" be taken into account? What are the implications of writing at this moment, in precisely this "America"? How to practice and make plural the written and spoken — grammars, syntaxes, textures, intonations . . .

Counter the potential totalizing power of language that serves the prevailing systems and demands of coherence

Contemplate the generative power of the designation "illegible" coming to speech

Enter language as it factors in, layers in, and crosses fields of meaning, elaborating and extending the possibilities for sense making

Consider how the polyglot, porous, transcultural presence alerts and alters what is around it

duration

"This is to be sung"
"This is to be done"

The lyric undertakes the task of deciphering and embodying a "particularizable" prosody of one's living.

And in that process, inside the procedures of work and of work proceeding: node and pressure point, song making and song gesture. Track: descant, sedimentations, tributaries in any several directions. Show stress, show beat, show alterations in pitch and accentuals. Tempo ruptured, emended. A valence of first and further tongues. Elements of the lyric and its mediations. The duration of the now, the now occurring, that manifests a time before.

A line's shape, vector, and motion interpolates perception and meter

A measure, a page, the book to embody the multivalent, the multidirectional —
a cathexis of the living instant to the acuteness of history

Each sound trace, each demonstration of the line, each formal enunciation: aperture: conduit: coming into articulation, into the Imaginary — the lyric as it embodies the processural

The poem may be said to reside in disrupted, dilated, circulatory spaces, and it is the means by which one notates this provisional location that evokes and demonstrates agency — the ear by which the prosody by which to calibrate the liberative potential of writing, storehouse of the human

To probe the terms under which we denote, participate in, and speak of cultural and human practices —

To mobilize the notion of our responsibility to one another in social space

Designer:	INA CLAUSEN
Compositor:	BOOKMATTERS
Text:	8.5/11 X 26 ELECTRA REGULAR AND CURSIVE
Display:	UNIVERS 57 CONDENSED, UNIVERS 57 CONDENSED OBLIQUE